Floral Watercolor

A BEGINNER'S GUIDE

WELCOME

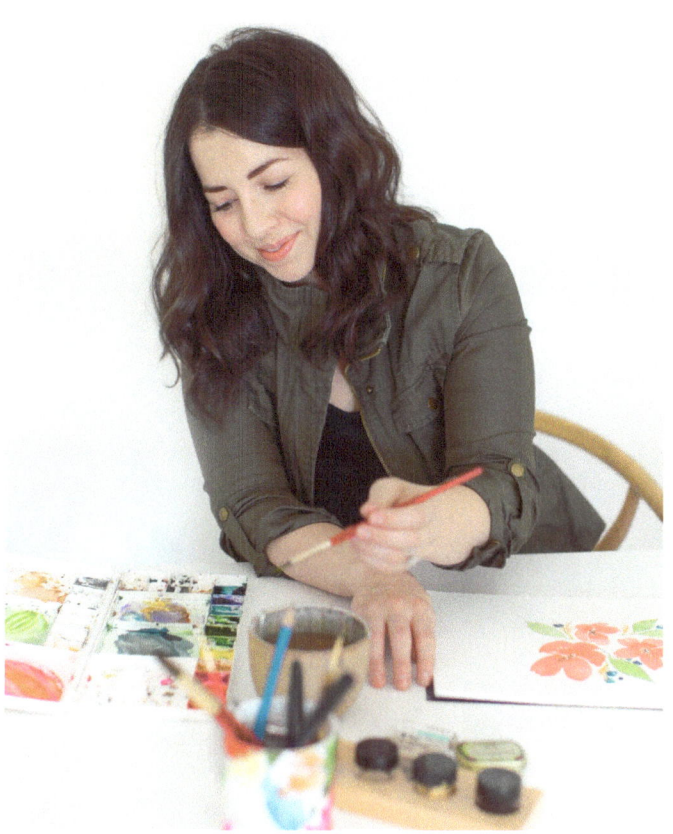

I'm so glad you're here!

Learning how to paint with watercolor has been a life changing experience for me – so much so that I had to share it with others. Since you are here, you probably already know watercolor painting to be a beautiful form of art, but did you know it is also used in conjunction with modern medicine to lower blood pressure, decrease anxiety, and cope with grief and loss? It truly is an amazing practice.

As you work through the pages of this booklet and become acquainted with this new form of art, I hope you are inspired, encouraged, and changed for the better. You have been provided with all the instruction you need, along with a list of all the supplies necessary to begin learning the basics of watercolor right away.

Let's get started!

— **AMANDA HOUSTON**

Table of
CONTENTS

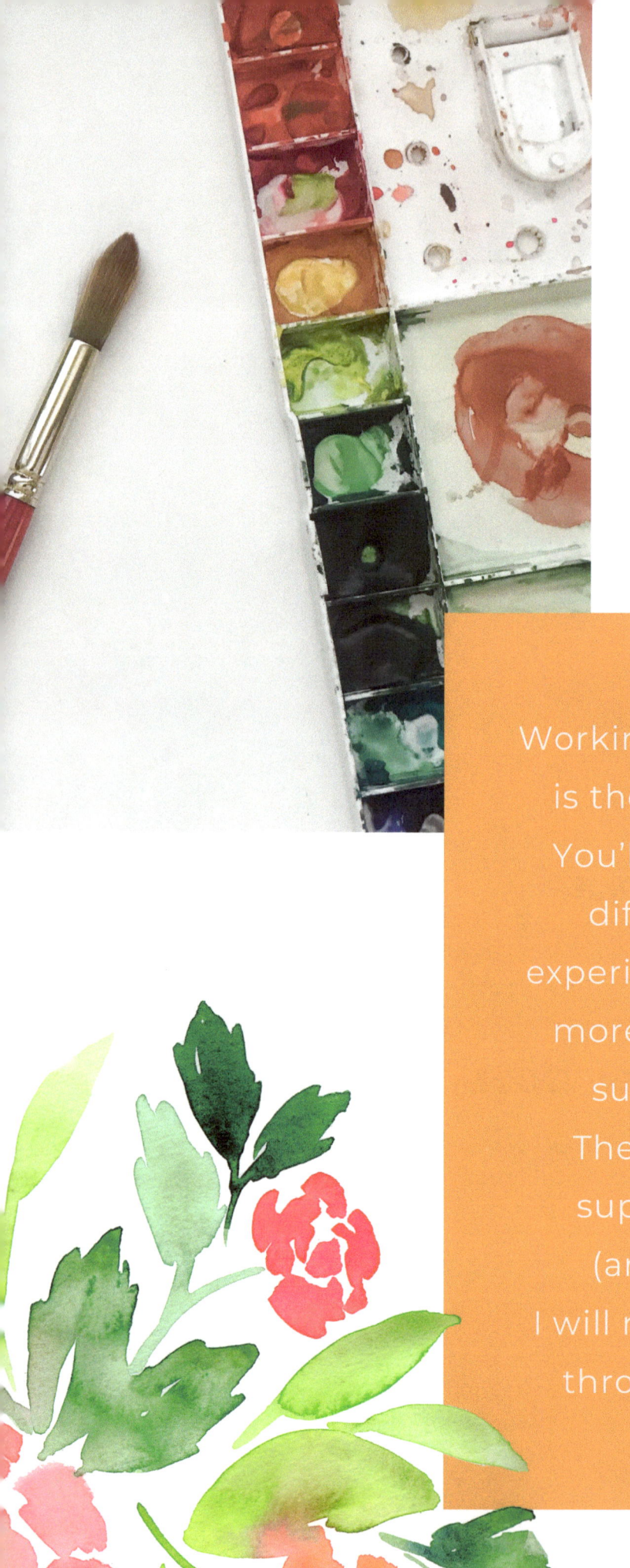

01

SUPPLIES

Working with quality supplies
is the best place to begin.
You'll be surprised at how
different the painting
experience can be as you are
more intentional with the
supplies you choose.
The following is a list of
supplies I recommend
(and use personally!)
I will refer to these regularly
throughout this booklet.

PROFESSIONAL GRADE WATERCOLOR PAINT

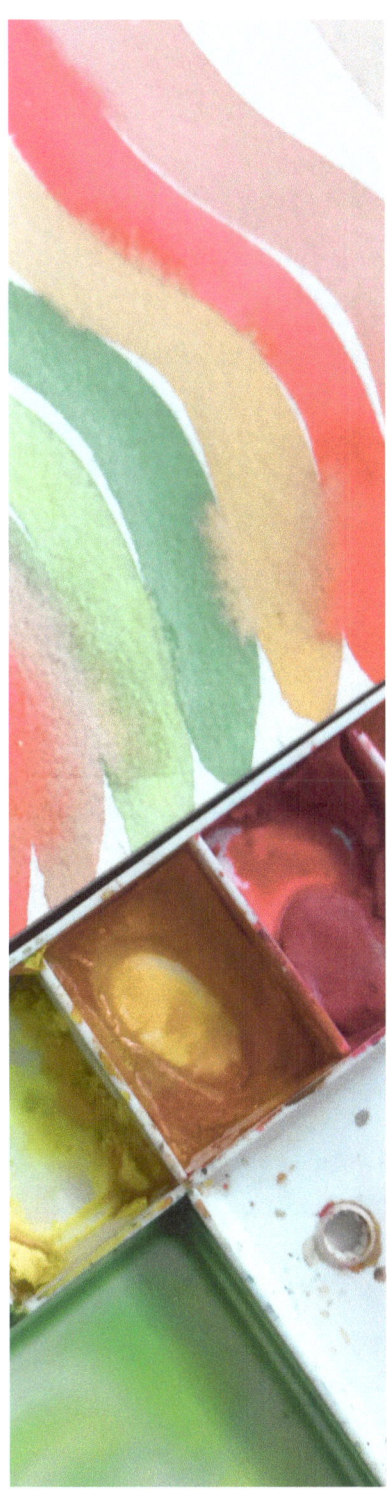

If you've never worked with professional grade watercolor before, you're in for a treat. Professional watercolor comes in tubes of wet paint, which we will add to our watercolor palette a little bit at a time. I personally love using the Winsor & Newton brand because I trust the quality, and the pigments are always so vibrant. You will notice the pigments in "professional" or "artist" grade paints are significantly more vibrant than a palette of dry paint, caked into pans, or "student" quality, and a little bit will go much further. Lesser quality paints have more binder and filler added to them, which results in less vibrancy. Professional grade paints will also dry with a nice finish, as opposed to cheaper paints that tend to dry chalk-like.

When working with tubes of watercolor paint, you want to squeeze the paint out into your paint wells about 24 hours before you're ready to paint. This is to ensure you don't pick up too much paint on your brush and waste it (since, like I said, a little bit goes a long way.) I recommend starting with the following paint colors from W&N (or similar colors from another professional brand): Prussian Blue, Olive Green, Lemon Yellow Deep, Scarlet Lake, Opera Rose, Ivory Black, and Magnesium Brown.

ROUND WATERCOLOR BRUSHES - VARIETY OF SIZES

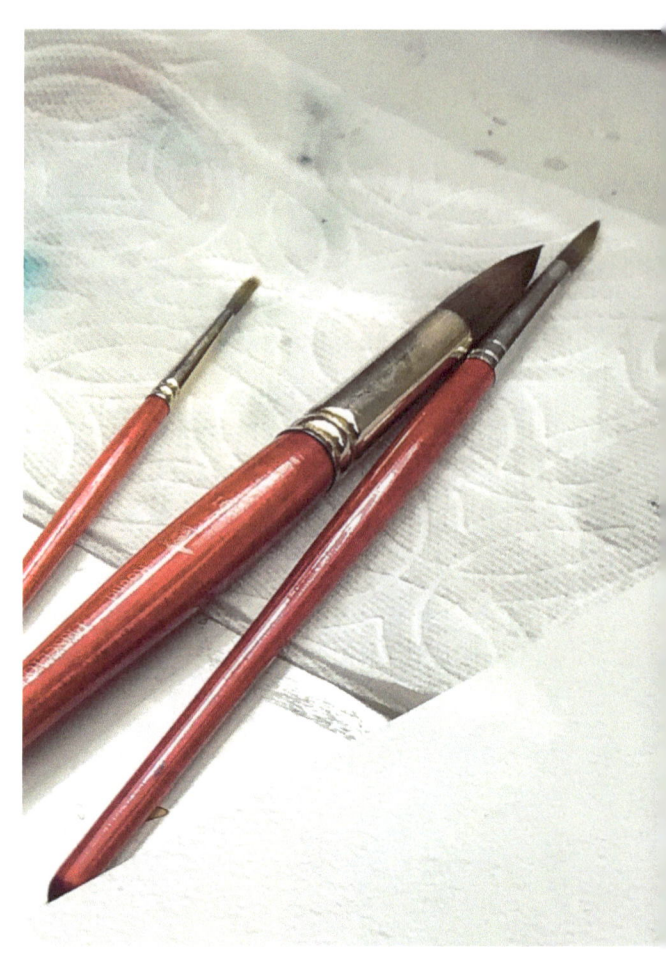

Round watercolor brushes are wonderful to paint with because of their versatility (which we will get more into soon,) and having a larger brush (around size 16) and a smaller brush (around size 6) will allow you to paint just about anything your heart desires. I recommend starting with the Princeton Snap series. When you feel you are ready for the next level, Princeton is a great brand to stick with, but you can move onto synthetic sable hair brushes (their Heritage series) as a step up. These are a little bit more pricey, so I recommend getting comfortable with beginner brushes first, since they are still great quality, and will produce wonderful results.

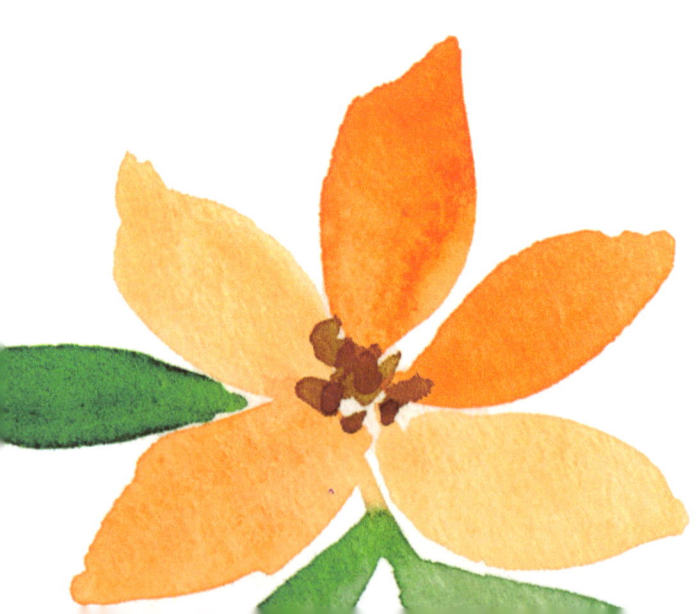

FIND WHAT MAKES YOU COME ALIVE AND DO IT.

COLD PRESSED WATERCOLOR PAPER

There are a few important things to keep in mind when selecting watercolor paper. First, 100% cotton paper is the most ideal as it will hold and absorb your paint better than anything else. Paper that is not 100% cotton can also tend to pill or become overworked easily. Second, you will want to use cold pressed paper rather than hot pressed paper, as it has more grooves so your paint doesn't pool on top of your paper. Finally, you'll want to work with at least 140lb./300gsm paper to minimize warping (the heavier the weight, the more water/paint it can hold.) My favorite brands for watercolor paper are Fluid 100, Arches, Legion, and Winsor and Newton.

And while all of these brands are the most ideal for a finished product, if you are just learning and practicing, a less expensive option is okay. Bear in mind, there will be a big difference in the results of your work when you use higher quality paper, so sometimes it's worth it to practice on the real thing.

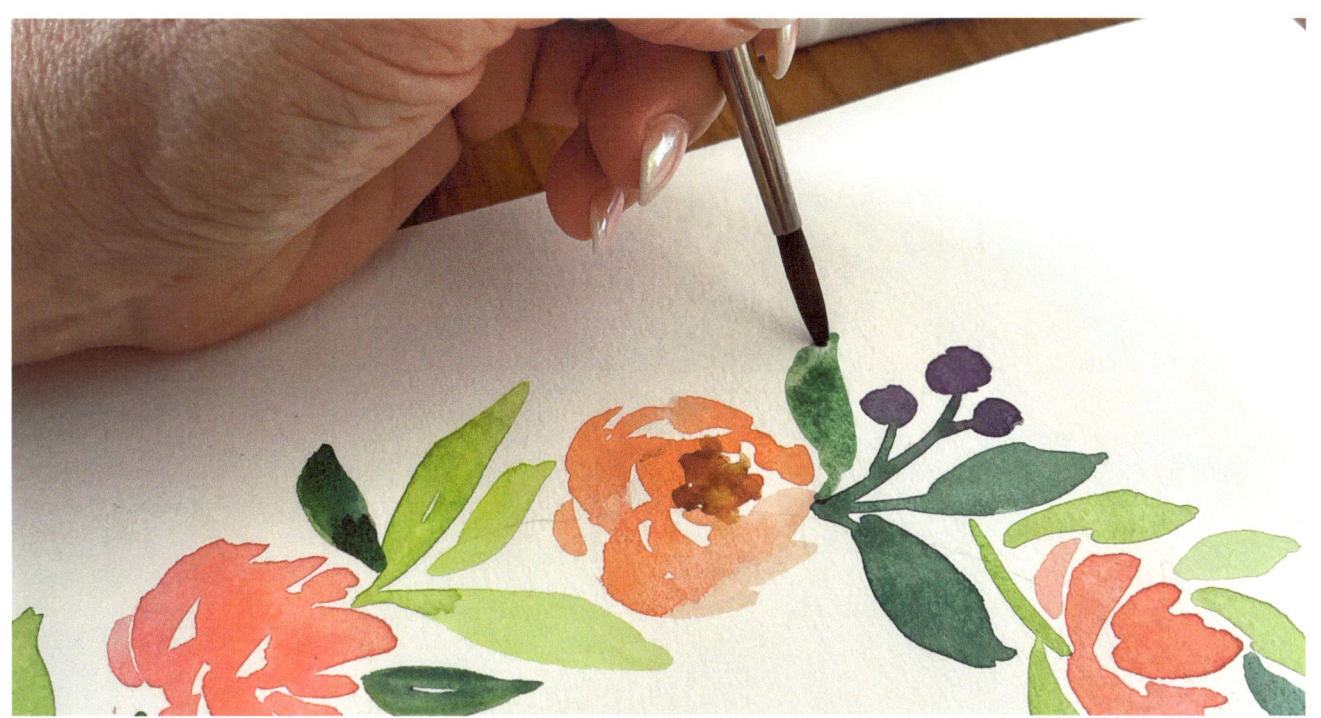

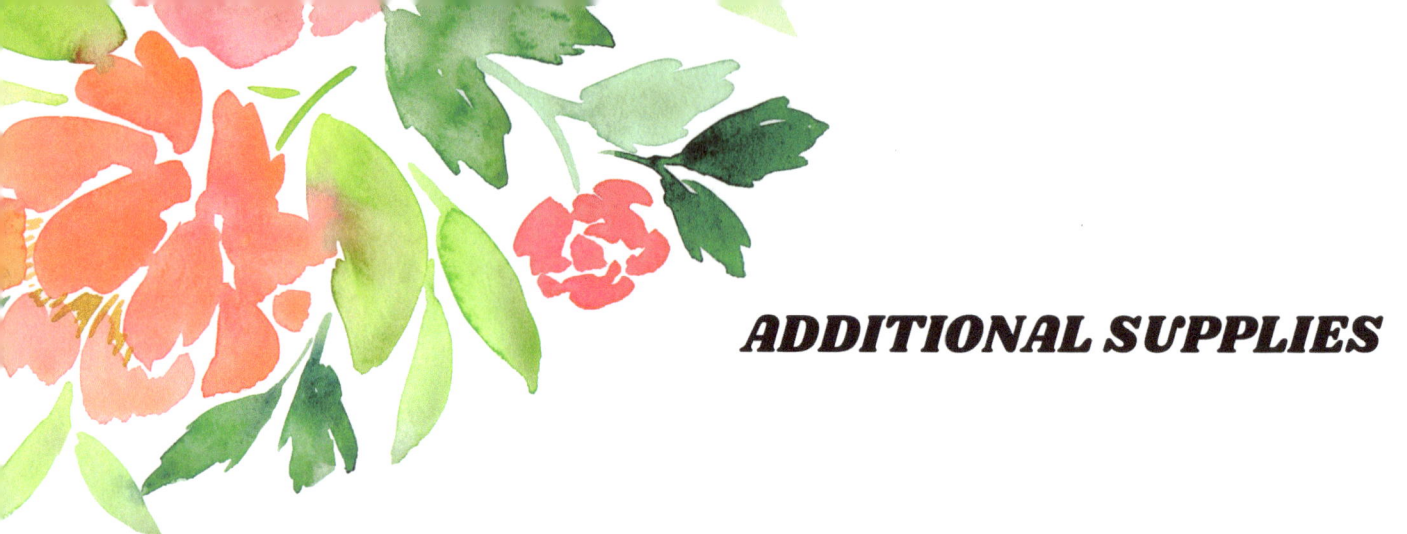

ADDITIONAL SUPPLIES

In addition to the supplies mentioned above, here are a few more items I recommend (some of them are probably already available in your home.)

Paint palette - if you do not already have a palette for your watercolor paint, you can find plastic palettes for a few dollars at any craft store. You'll want to make sure there is plenty of space (in addition to the paint wells) so you can mix your paint.

Watercolor pencil - I love using a light grey watercolor pencil when laying out a piece before painting. You will not always need to layout first, but if you do, this is a great tool to use, as the lines will simply fade into your painting once exposed to water (regular pencil cannot be erased once painted over.)

Watercolor Wheel - this is a helpful tool for understanding how colors mix, and how you can achieve a broader range of color from even a small palette of paint colors.

Paper towels - for absorbing excess water from your brush or painting.

Water dish - whatever you're most comfortable working with to rinse your brushes as you work.

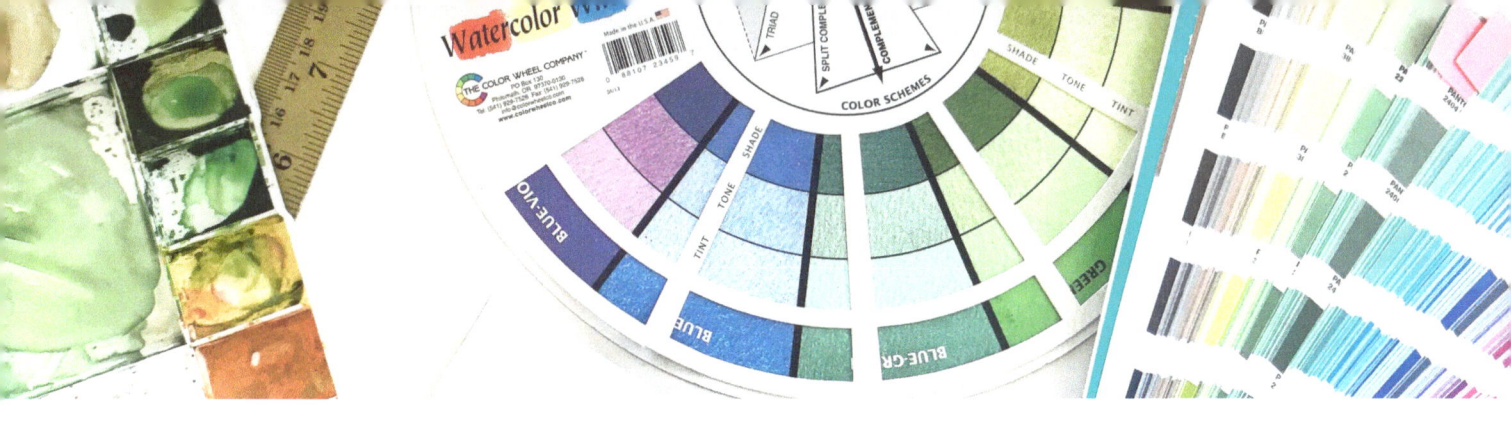

RECOMMENDED SUPPLY LIST

 Winsor & Newton Professional Watercolor (or Cotman series) - Select a variety of hues. A good starting point is as follows: Prussian Blue, Olive Green, Lemon Yellow Deep, Scarlet Lake, Opera Rose, Ivory Black, and Magnesium Brown.

 Princeton (Snap Series) Watercolor Brushes - Select at least 2 sizes of round brushes. Sizes 6 and 16 is a great starting point.

 Cold-Pressed Watercolor Paper - Select paper that is 100% cotton and at least 140lb weight. Good brands are Global Fluid 100, Arches, Legion Stonehenge Aqua, and Winsor & Newton.

 Paint Palette - Watercolor palettes come in all shapes, sizes, and materials. Choose what works best within your budget. A plastic palette will be the most affordable option.

 Watercolor Pencil - I like to keep a grey watercolor pencil on hand for pieces that require sketching before painting.

 Watercolor Wheel - Helps as you grow in your understanding of color theory, and how to mix colors properly.

CHA PTER TWO

THE BASICS

Learn more about the basics of color, mixing, bleed, and additional techniques that will be the foundation for painting beautiful florals.

COLOR

Watercolor paint is an extremely versatile medium, and is actually quite forgiving as you become more familiar with it. As I mentioned before, when you are using high quality paints, the pigments will be very strong, so you can produce a wide range of color intensity by simply adding (or taking away) water. When selecting colors to work with, remember that colors can always be toned down with a little black or brown, but you can never brighten dull colors. That is why your palette is filled mostly with pure, vibrant color. Let's begin with an exercise to help understand this concept.

Grab your size 16 brush and dip it in your water. For the first use you'll notice a light seal on the brush that will go away as you press it down in the base of your water dish. Select a color, and press the side of the well with your brush to add water to the paint well. Swirl your brush in the paint until the water is highly concentrated with pigment, and fill your paintbrush with the paint. Lightly touch the edge of your well to remove any paint drips, and paint a small swatch on your paper by gently pressing your brush to the paper at a slight angle (see example below). Do not re-dip in your paint. Instead, dip once in water, and tap the side of your water dish to gently remove excess water, then paint another swatch right next to the previous. Continue to repeat these steps, dipping only in water, until the pigment is no longer visible. This exercise shows the variety in lightness and darkness of pigment that can be achieved by simply adding water.

Unlike with other mediums, there is no need to add white paint to your watercolor in order to achieve a lighter color. Adding white paint will only dull your pigment, thus defeating the purpose of buying such quality paint. By simply adding water, you can make any given color as light (or dark) as you would like. Remember as you paint, water is your friend, and as long as it is not pooling on top of your paper, wet is a good thing. If you paint with the right amount of water, a thin, dark drying line should appear just around the edges of each shape once they have dried.

Now, continue this same exercise with each of the colors in your palette to get familiar with them.

COLOR MIXING

As you experiment with the colors in your palette, you may be concerned with the limited amount of hues, and wishing you had more colors to work with. This is where basic knowledge of color comes in handy (think back to elementary school here!) We know the basics, like red and yellow makes orange, blue and yellow makes green, red and blue makes purple, but did you know you can produce a beautiful burgundy with red and a little bit of black? I told you watercolor is a very versatile medium, and I truly meant it! The reality is, by simply mixing some of the colors in your palette, you will be able to produce more colors than you will know what to do with. You simply have to spend a little time getting to know your palette better. Based on the 7 colors I recommended you begin with, you already have access to a minimum of 49 colors by simply mixing any given two colors together. If you mix more than 2 colors, there are even more possibilities! So, let's begin with some basic mixtures.

Using the same technique we learned to create our swatches, begin by filling your brush with one paint color, and adding it to one of the empty paint wells by pressing it to the side of the well. Rinse your brush, then do the same thing with the second color, adding it to the same well. Swirl your brush around until the paint has fully mixed, then paint a swatch on your paper to see the beautiful result. You can adjust the hue by adding more of one color or the other. Try each of the examples below, then experiment with some of your own combinations.

OPERA ROSE AND LEMON YELLOW DEEP

SCARLET LAKE AND IVORY BLACK

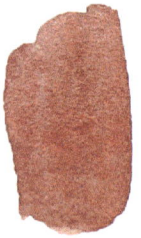

PRUSSIAN BLUE AND OLIVE GREEN

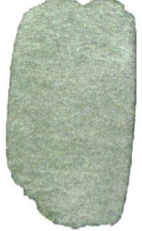

OLIVE GREEN AND MAGNESIUM BROWN

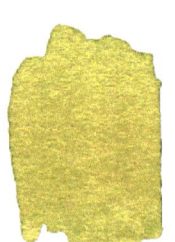

OPERA ROSE AND PRUSSIAN BLUE

COLOR BLEED

Now that we understand a little bit more about how colors mix together, I want to introduce you to one of my favorite aspects of watercolor: color bleed. A bleed occurs when two different areas of wet pigment touch, causing the stronger, more vibrant pigment, to "bleed" into the other (see example above.) To practice a color bleed, paint a swatch of one color, rinse your brush, then select another color. Now here's the important part – paint your second swatch right next to the other, but very slowly, and just barely, touch the two colors together. As long as both swatches are wet, you should see an explosion of color. Continue to play with different colors, and notice how some pigments overtake others. Just make sure you work quickly, as this will not work with a dry swatch. Keep making swatches, connecting each one to the last, until your page is full of an abstract work of art.

BRUSH TECHNIQUE

Now that we have a better understanding of how our watercolor paint works, and how it interacts with our brushes and paper, we can begin to learn a little more technique with our brushes.

Grab your size 6 (or smaller) brush, and fill it with a color of your choice. Holding your brush perpendicular to your paper, (straight up and down, with just the tip touching your paper) paint a line (see example below.)

Using the same brush, adjust your angle to about 45 degrees and add a slight amount of pressure as you paint another line.

Now change your angle one more time to be closer to about 25 degrees, add even more pressure, and paint a third line.

You should now have 3 lines of differing thickness, all produced from the same brush. Continue to practice drawing lines of different thickness to become more acquainted with your brush and what it is a capable of, by changing your angle and pressure. Use your size 16 (or larger) brush for the same exercise.

SIZE 6 BRUSH

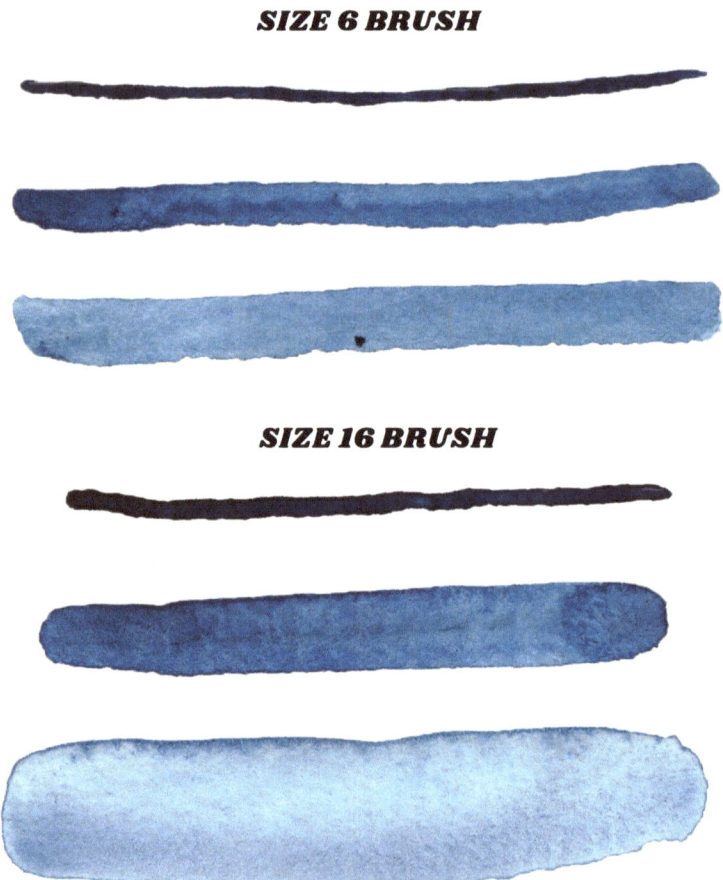

SIZE 16 BRUSH

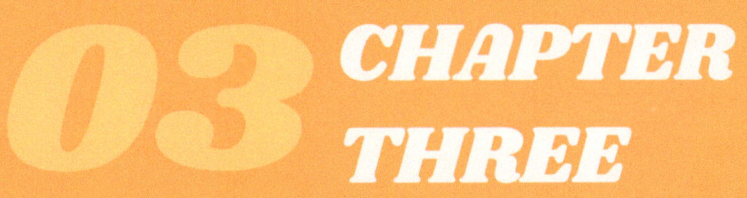

03 CHAPTER THREE

FLORALS

Now that you've learned basic watercolor techniques, and understand a little bit more about how your materials work, we're ready to begin learning some basic loose florals.

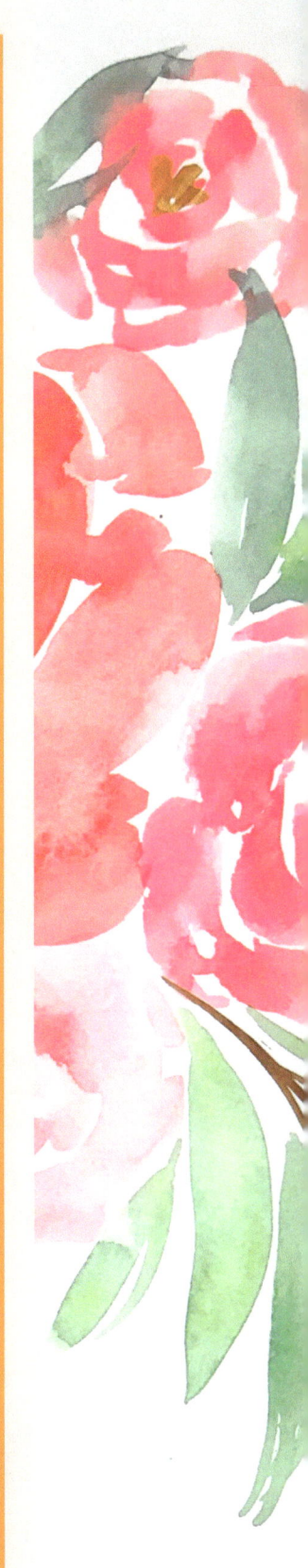

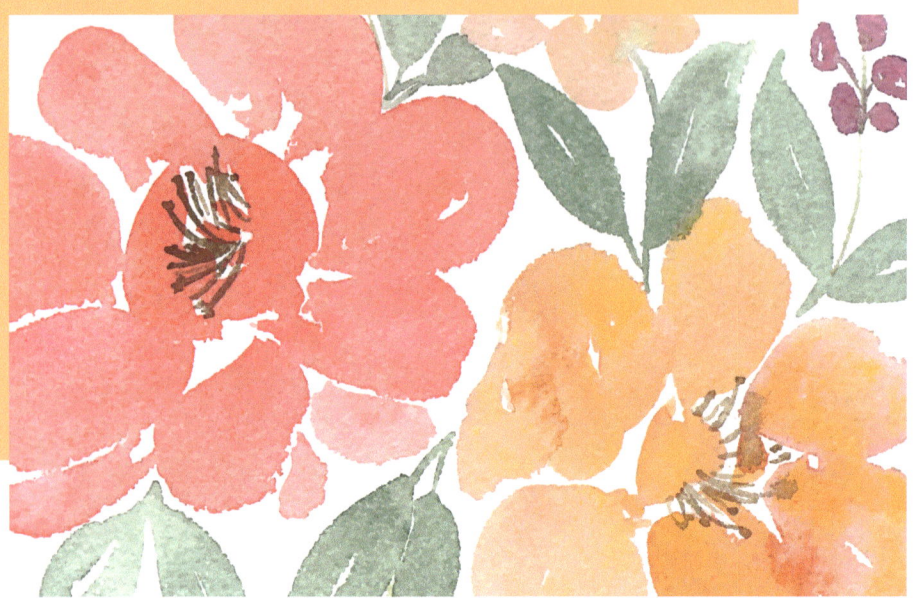

When painting florals with watercolor, there are a variety of styles to choose from. For a more literal approach, you will need to sketch out your floral piece first, then fill it in utilizing shading techniques to make a more realistic piece. This is a more advanced approach that also requires some basic drawing knowledge.

What we will be learning in this booklet is how to paint "loose florals." This is an abstract approach to floral watercolor, and is great for anyone who is just beginning to learn. In this booklet, I will go over two different types of flowers, and two different types of leaves, step by step. At the end of this section, you will also find a page full of floral examples, and a page full of leaf examples for you to try with your new skills.

start where you are

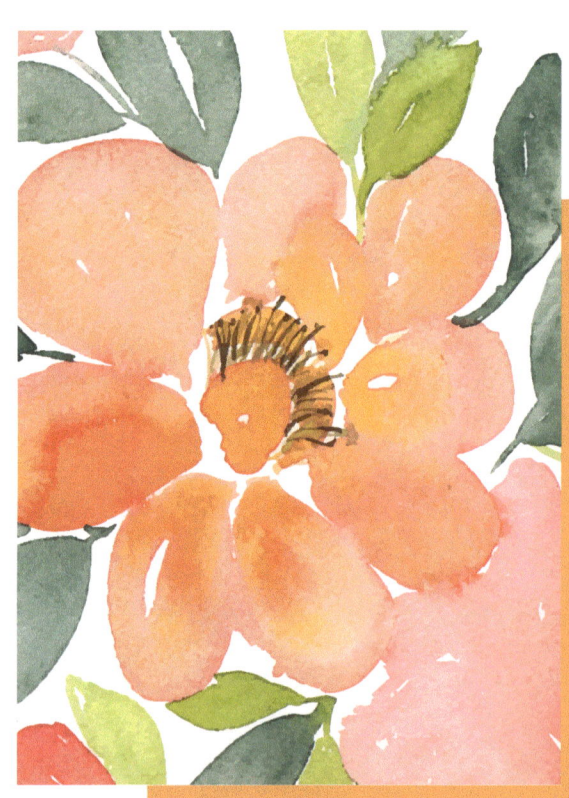

PAINTING THE ROSE

To paint a rose (from an over top viewpoint,) we start in the center, with your brush held perpendicular to your paper to produce thinner lines. Select a color, fill your brush with that color, and begin by making a few staggered "c" shapes to mimic the tight center of a rose (step 1.) Leave a small circular space in the center for stamen, and plenty of white space throughout, so it doesn't look like one blob of color. Slowly start to lower the angle of your brush and add more pressure as you work outward to make increasingly larger petals (steps 2-4.) As you feel your brush beginning to dry, dip lightly in water (not paint,) tap the excess off the side of your water dish, and continue working. This will give your flower a little bit more of a realistic look, as most flowers are not exactly the same color throughout. After you've finished off the outer petals, make sure the paint in the center is still slightly wet, but not too wet, then select a yellowish/brown hue for the center stamen, and lightly dot the stamen in the center of your flower. Add additional petals to the outside to give your rose a finished/fuller look (step 5.) Add color to areas that need a little "pop" by adding more paint to your brush and gently dabbing it in the wet areas. The water will allow the paint to disperse naturally throughout your painting. Follow the step-by-step examples below to practice painting a rose.

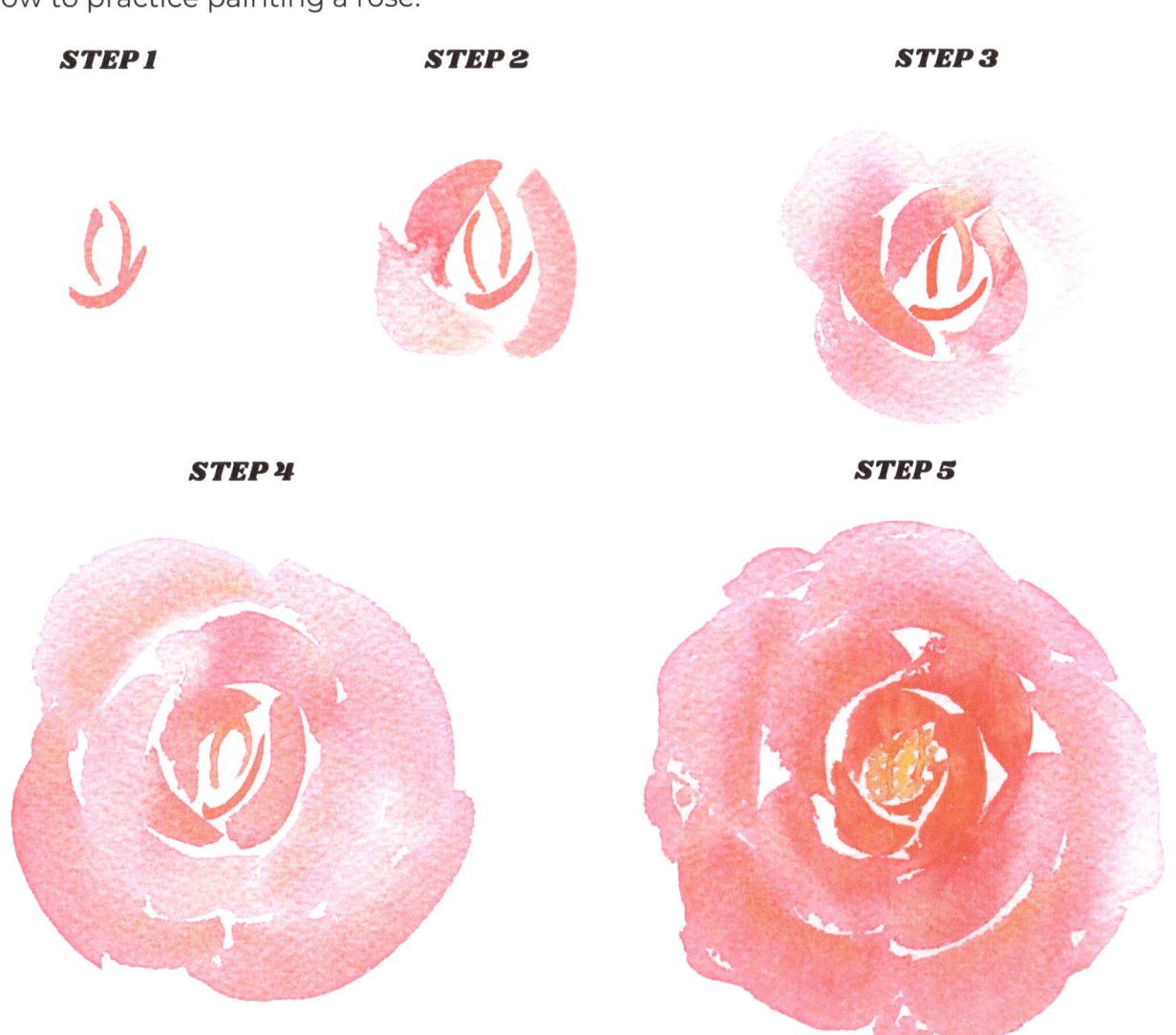

STEP 1   STEP 2   STEP 3

STEP 4   STEP 5

PAINTING THE PEONY

For the peony, you can approach from an angle similar to the rose we just painted, or you can approach it from a side angle. This is the angle we will be practicing for this example. To begin, envision your flower from the side. Imagine there is a sphere in the center that all the petals will gather around. Then, follow the steps in the example below. Start with tear drop-shaped petals, meeting at the bottom and blooming outward (steps 1-3.) To acheive this look, start with the point of your brush at the base of the petal, and create an upside down tear drop by rotating your brush in a semi-circular motion. Peony petals tend to have rough edges, so don't worry about making the petals perfectly rounded. Continue to build your flower in this fashion. Next, add some petals that appear to be falling outward (step 4,) followed be a few petals in the back of the flower (step 5,) with a little bit of white space for your stamen. Keep in mind, white space is your friend with loose florals. After your petals have dried slightly, use the tip of your brush to produce thin stamen, blooming out from the center (step 6.) Follow the step-by-step examples below to practice painting the peony. The same "tear drop" technique can be applied to create a peony from varying angles. Just keep plenty of white space between petals, and have fun!

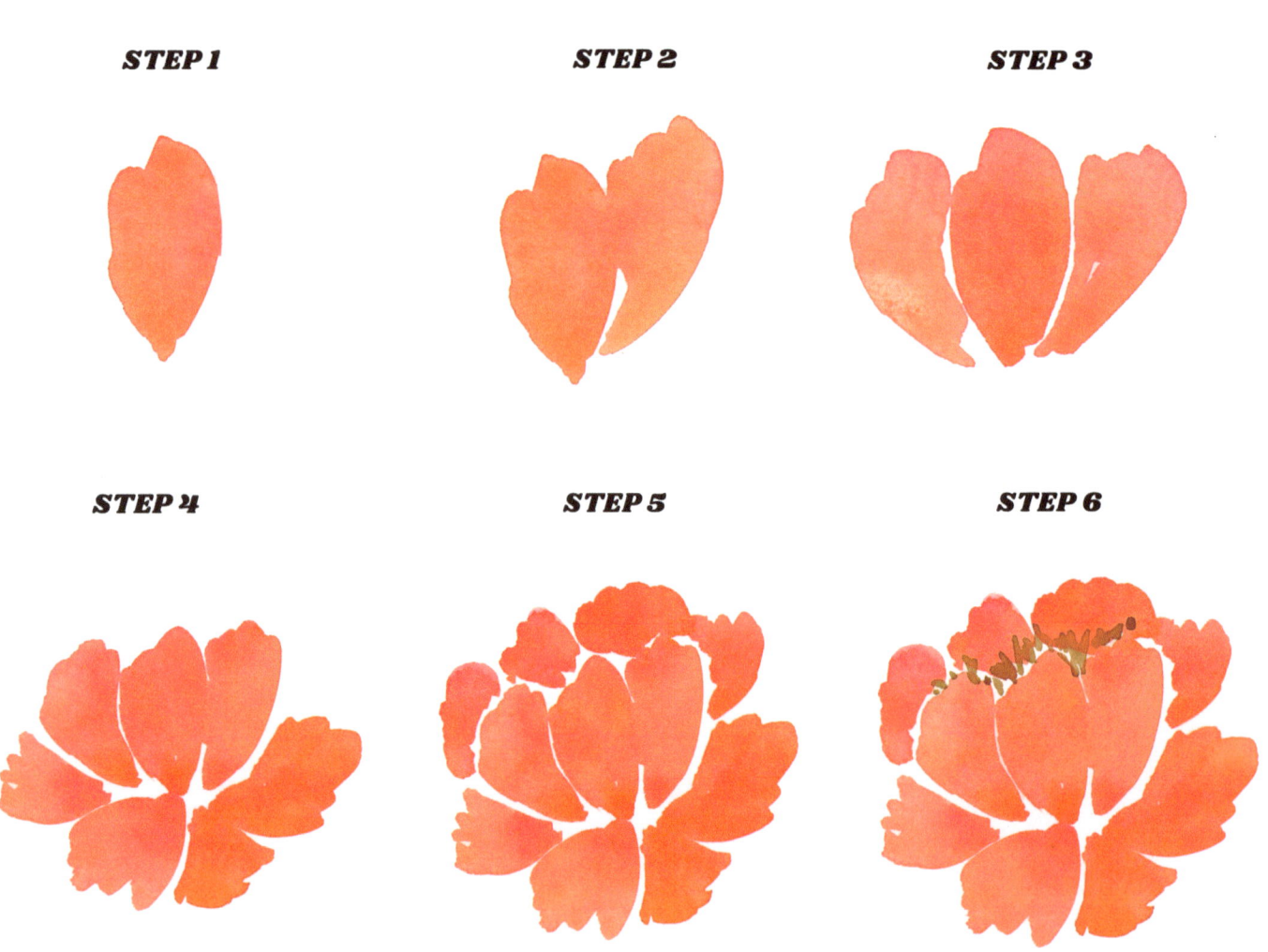

STEP 1   STEP 2   STEP 3

STEP 4   STEP 5   STEP 6

PAINTING ROSE LEAVES

Now we're going to learn two of the most common leaves you'll use with loose floral painting. The first is a rose leaf. Following the example below, paint a thin line to create the stem of your leaf (step 1.) Continuing from the base, begin with light pressure, then transition to a heavier amount of pressure, lowering the angle of your brush, then back to light pressure and a higher angle, to create one side of your leaf (step 2.) Do the same for the other side, bringing the tip of your two sides together to create a leaf (step 3.) While it is still wet, add some rough texture to the edges to give a more realistic look for the rose leaves (step 4.) Connect as many leaves as you'd like by first drawing a long stem, then adding leaves all along the stem (step 5.) Feel free to leave a little bit of white space in the center for natural highlighting. Now that you've got this down, add some leaves to your flowers. Keep in mind all leaves are not created equal. Your florals will look much more realistic if your leaves vary in size and color. So don't be afraid to change it up. Follow the step-by-step examples below to practice painting rose leaves.

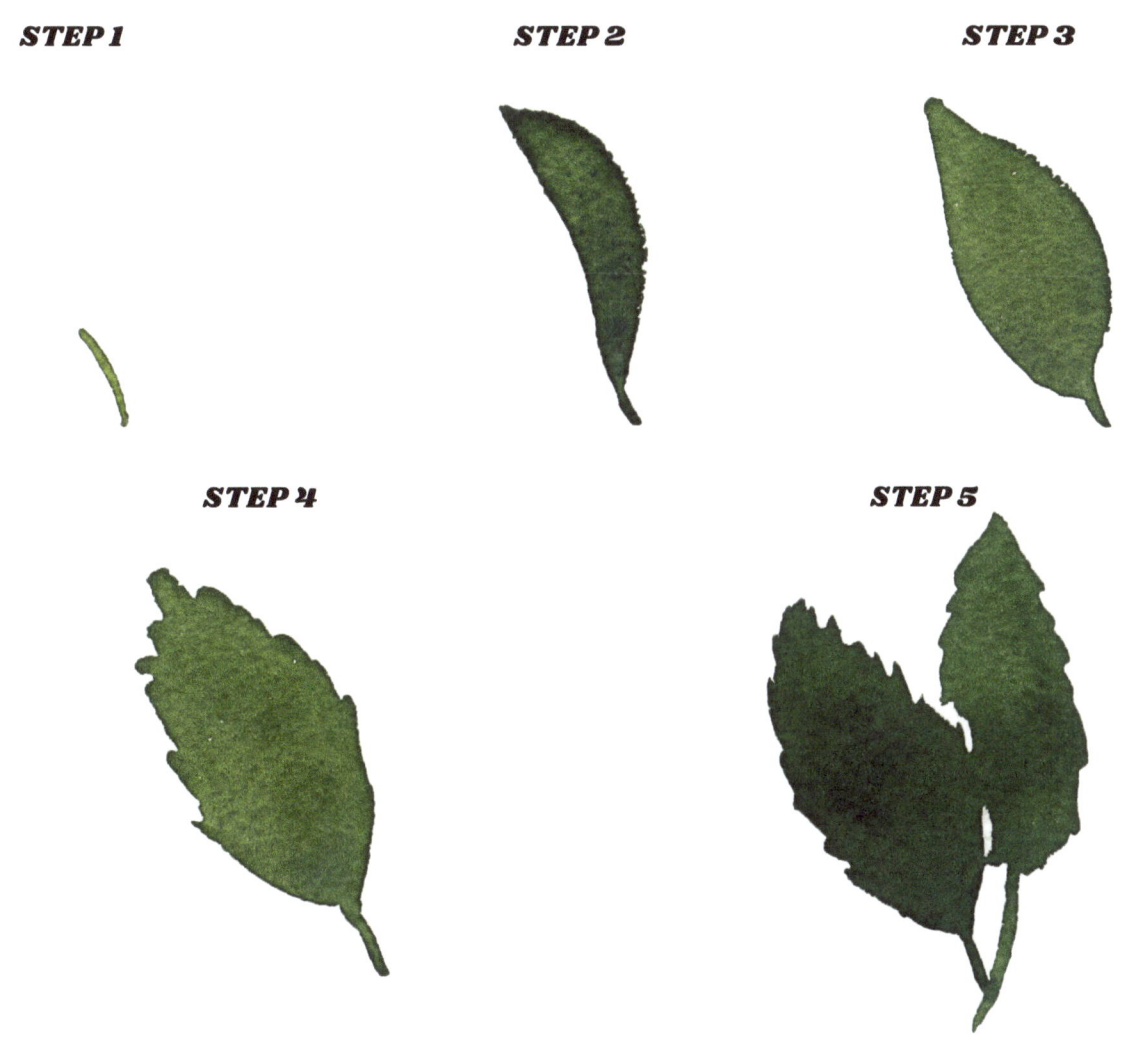

STEP 1   STEP 2   STEP 3

STEP 4   STEP 5

PAINTING PEONY LEAVES

The second leaf we are going to learn is very similar to the rose leaf. The main difference with peony leaves is they are longer and thinner, without the rough edges you will find on a rose leaf. Following the example on the next page, paint a thin line to create the stem of your leaf (step 1.) Continuing, begin with light pressure, then transition to a slightly heavier amount of pressure, just slightly lowering the angle of your brush, then back to light pressure and a higher angle, to create one side of your leaf (step 2.) Do the same for the other side, bringing the tip of your two sides together to create a leaf (step 3.) Continue to practice this leaf style by first drawing a long stem, then adding leaves all along the stem (step 4.) Follow the step-by-step examples below to practice painting peony leaves.

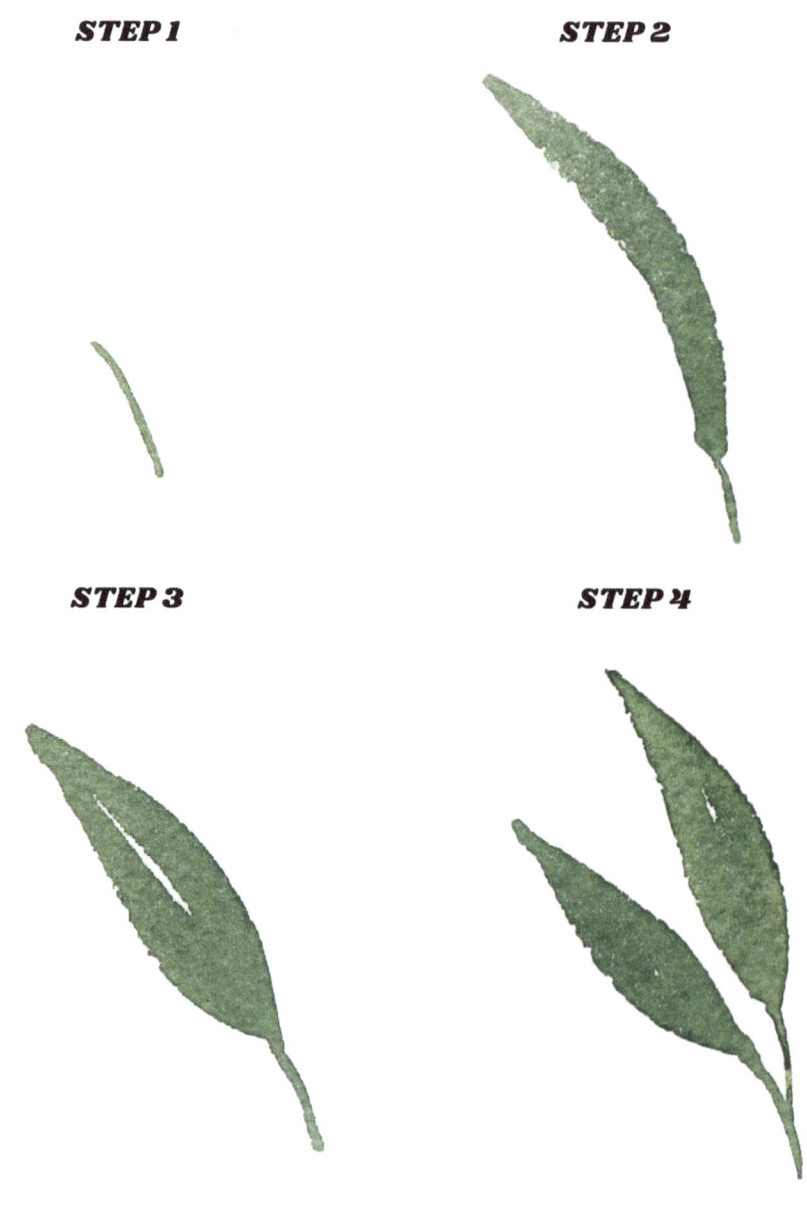

STEP 1   STEP 2

STEP 3   STEP 4

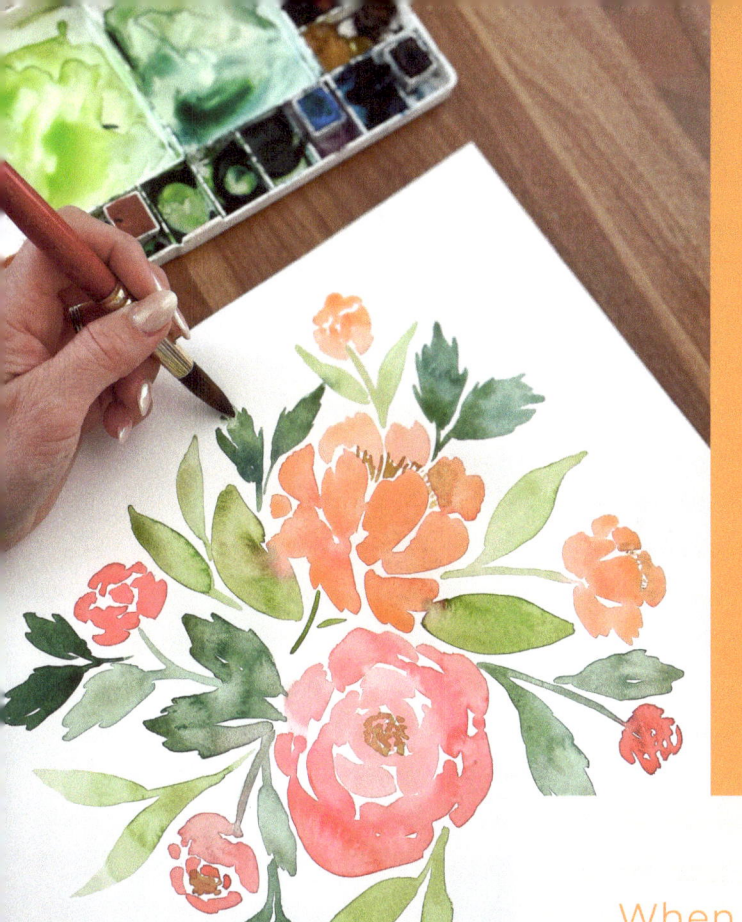

PRACTICE MAKES PROGRESS "

When it comes to painting florals, the best inspiration is nature. I recommend looking at actual flowers or photos of flowers as you paint, to help inform your placement of the petals and leaves. And most importantly, embrace the imperfections of nature as you practice your new skills.

Now that you've learned some basic florals, we'll apply what you've learned to try a variety of florals. Take a look at some of the examples on the following pages, and give them a try for yourself!

ADDITIONAL FLORAL EXAMPLES

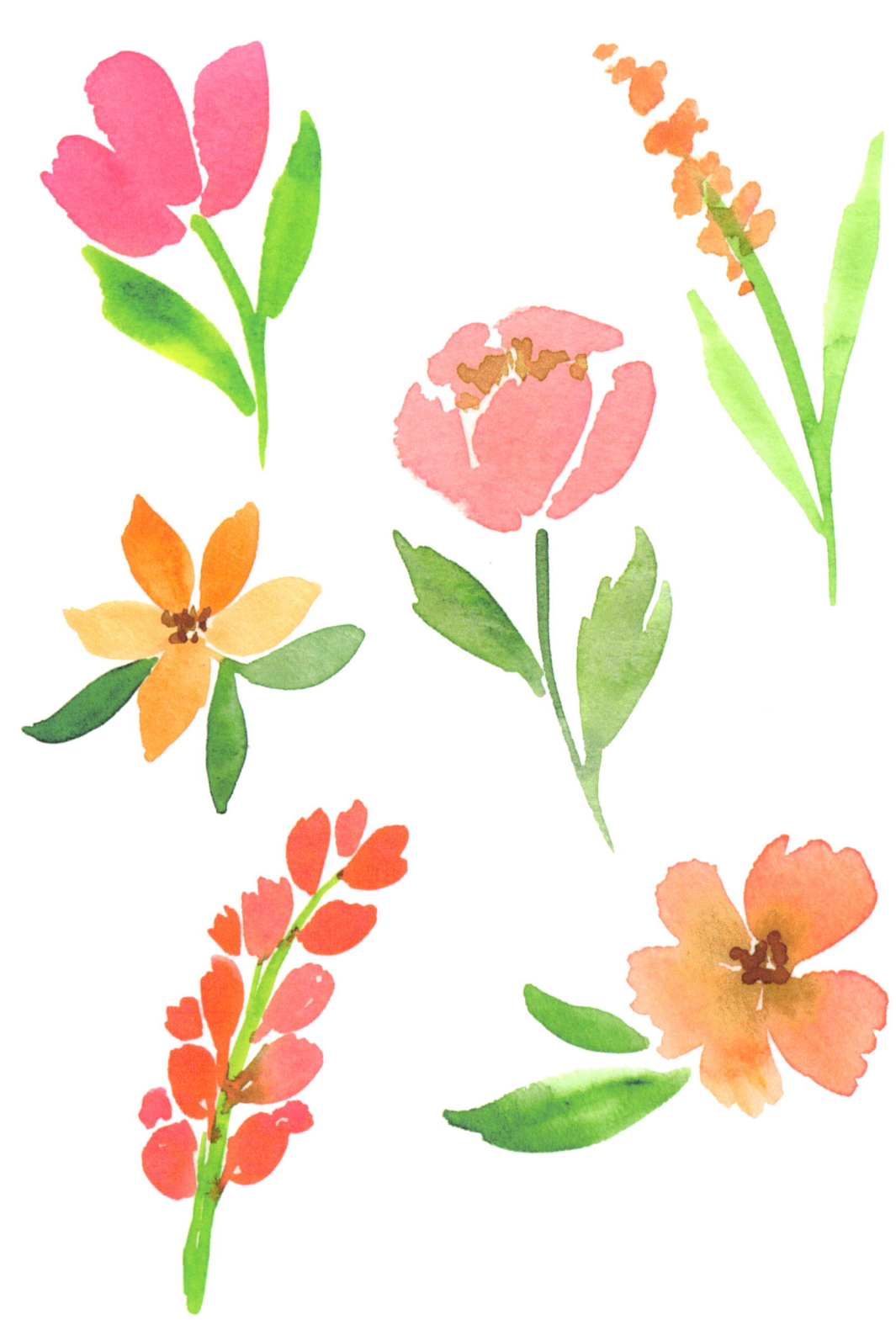

ADDITIONAL LEAF EXAMPLES

04

BRINGING IT TOGETHER

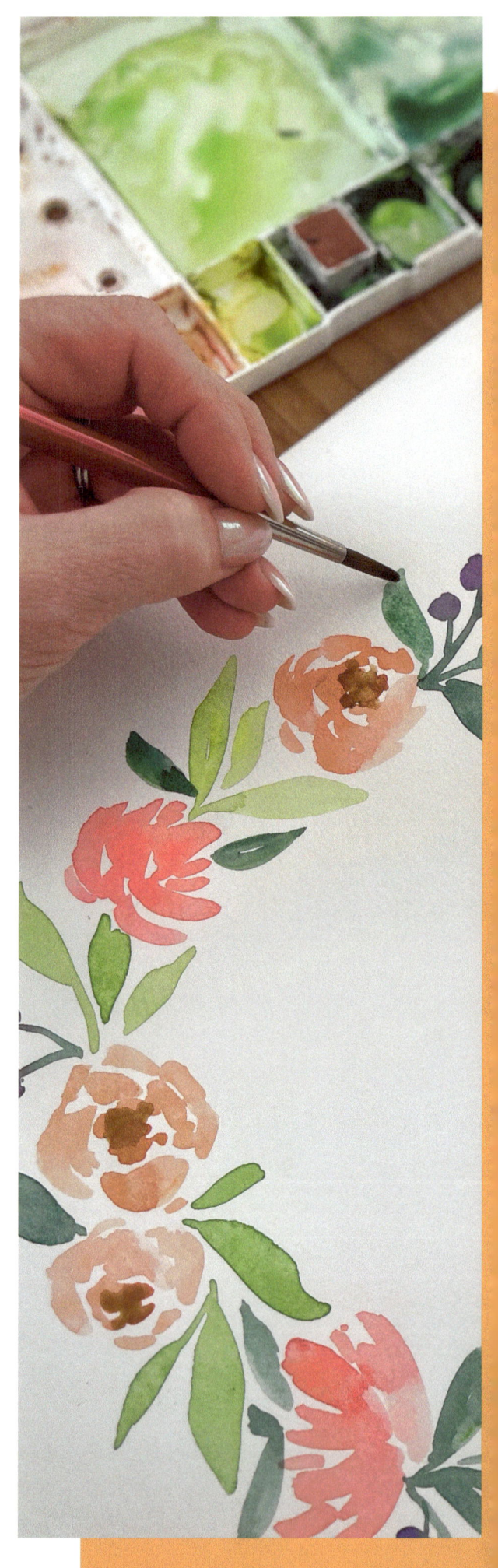

Now that you've learned the basic principles of floral watercolor, let's bring these concepts together by painting both a floral wreath and an arrangement utilizing each of the elements we've just learned (examples on the following pages.)

Don't be afraid to bring a little bit of your own style into this, but use the examples provided to help understand the basic composition of floral arrangement.

You may want to begin by copying the examples provided to get a feel for things.

Keep in mind, nature is not symmetrical, and odd numbers tend to look more balanced when it comes to composition. The more you practice, the more your artistic eye will develop to understand what is balanced, and what is not.

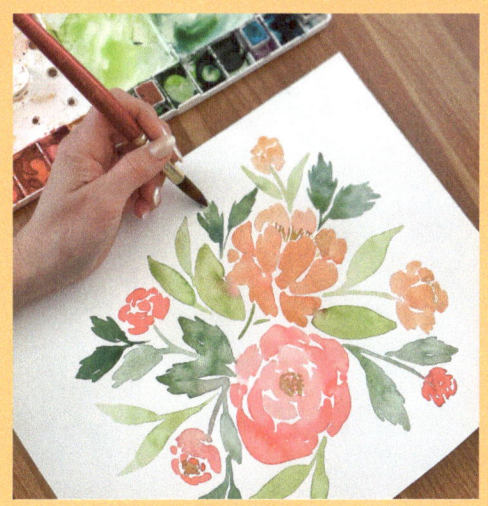

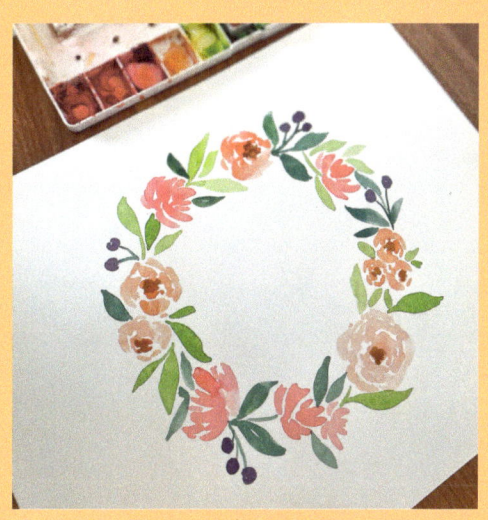

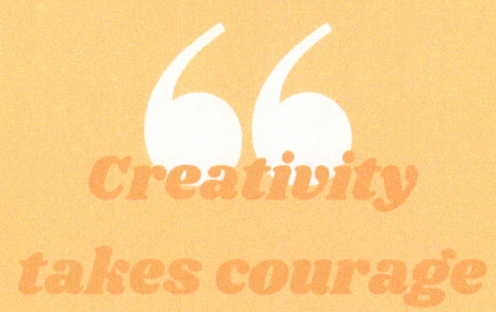

Creativity takes courage

PAINTING A FLORAL WREATH

A good floral wreath will have a variety of larger florals, leaves, and buds. Start by drawing a light circle guide well within your watercolor paper, so there is plenty of room for the florals to go outside the border of the circle as well. Then, begin with your flowers first. Space your flowers by color, size, and type, so there is variation. Then add your leaves. Once you've added leaves to the flowers, you can begin to examine what it needs to be complete in your eyes. This is where you can add any additional filler leaves, berries, or flower buds. Copy the example below for practice.

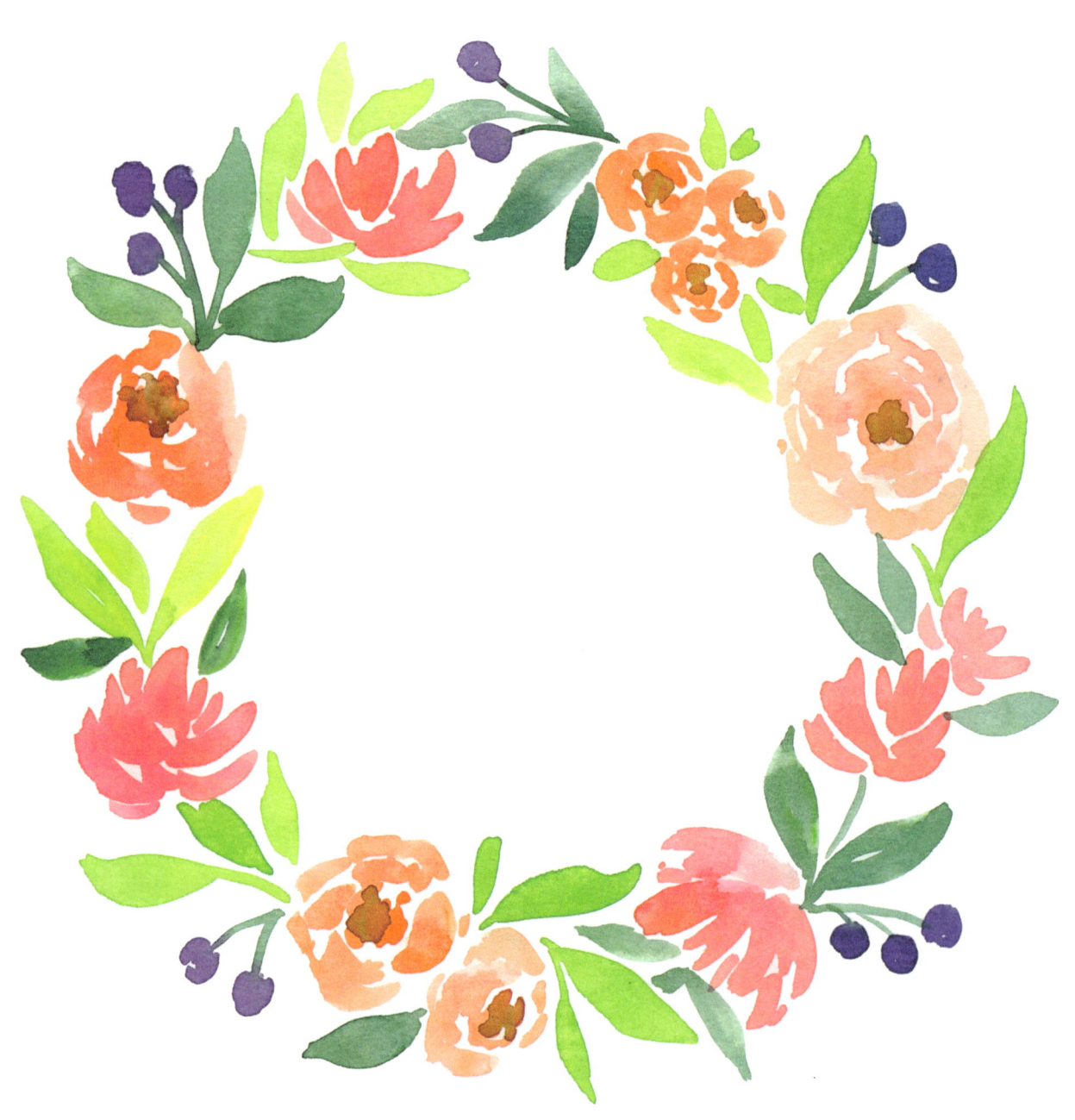

PAINTING A FLORAL ARRANGEMENT

Similar to the floral wreath, arrangements typically begin by placing the large flowers first. This will be your focal point. Then you may begin to fill in with smaller buds, berries, and leaves, as you desire. I like to imagine a floral arrangement like a bouquet of flowers I am looking at from the top down. Using photo references of real flower arrangements can be helpful too. Copy the example below for practice.

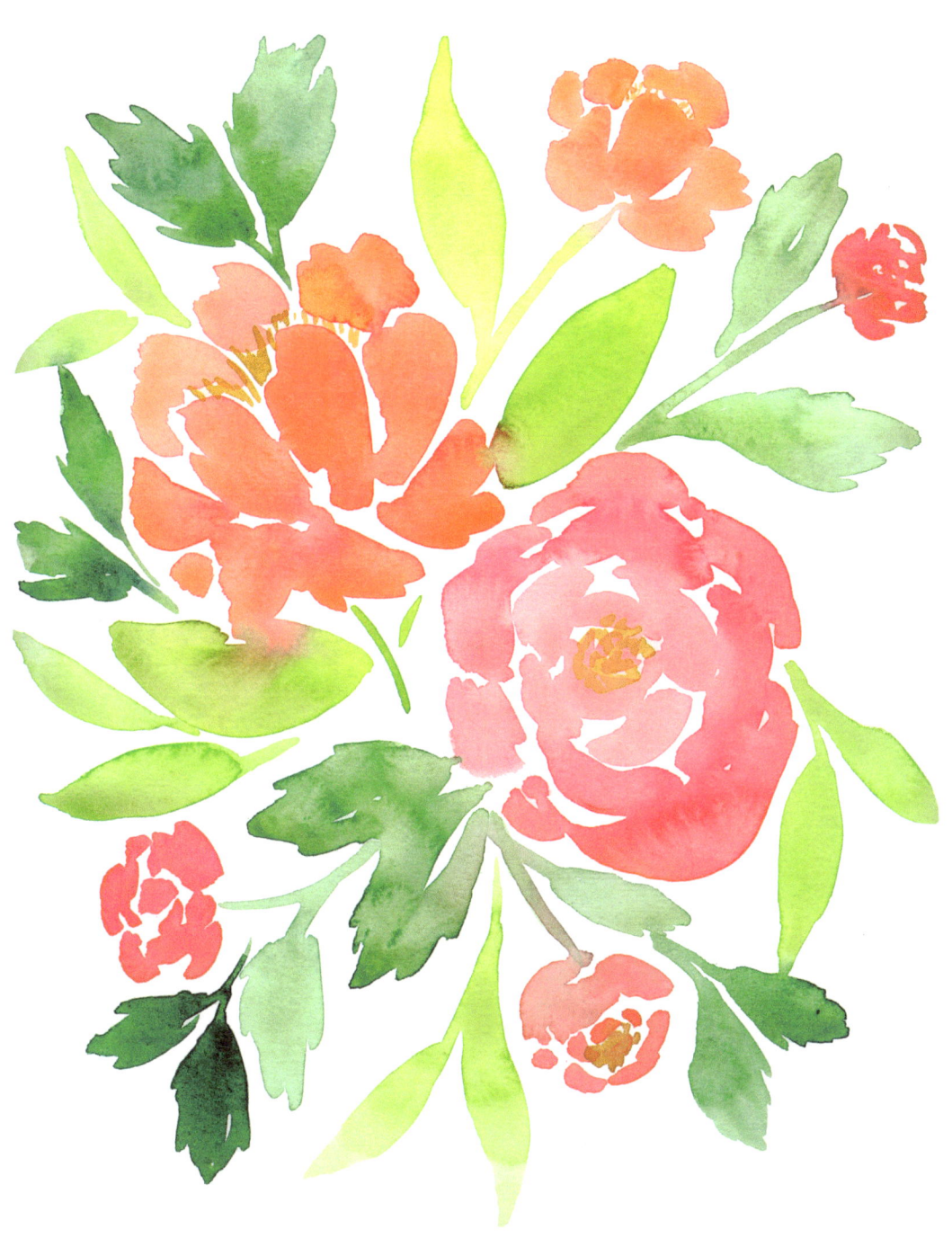

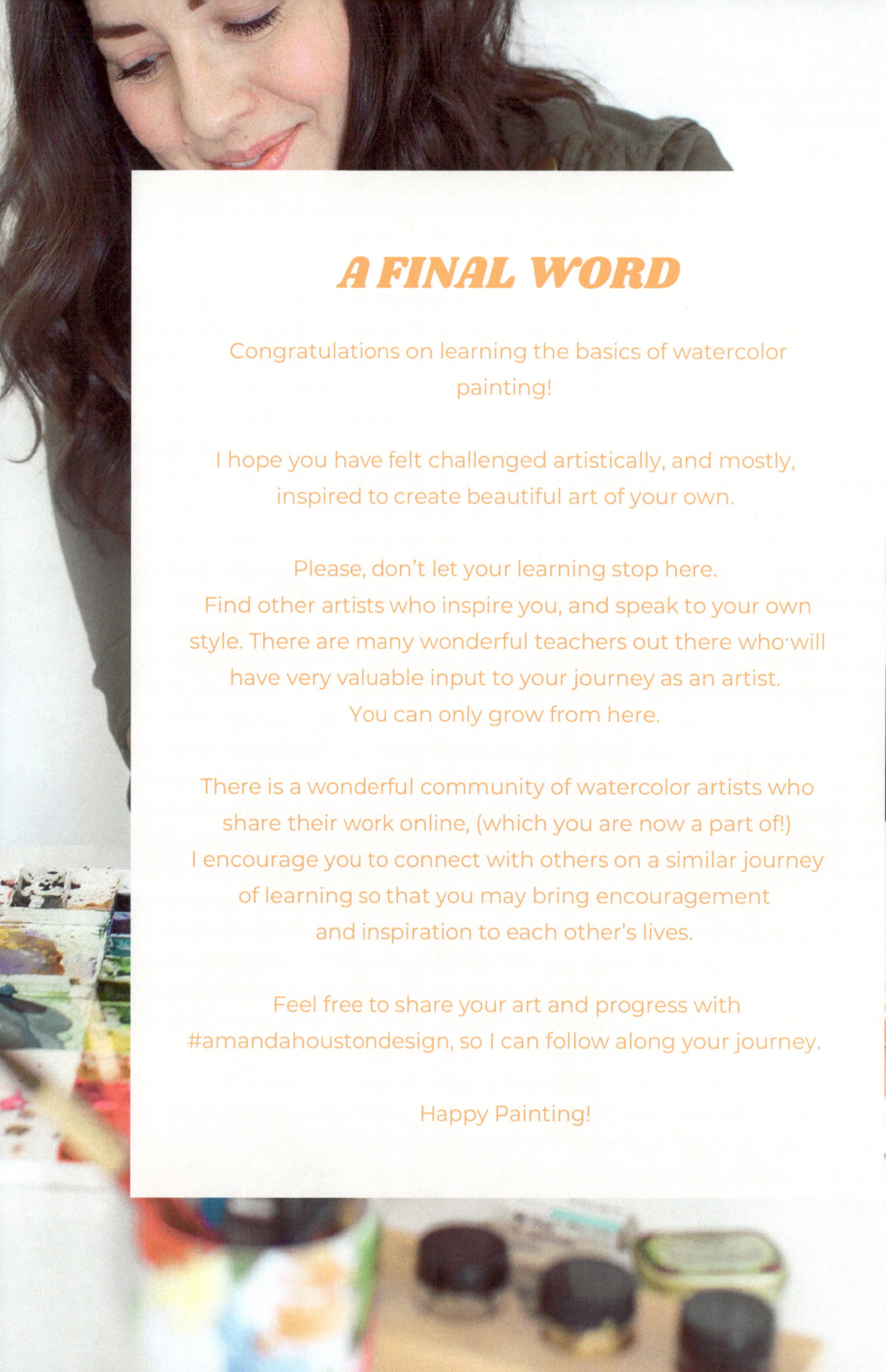

A FINAL WORD

Congratulations on learning the basics of watercolor painting!

I hope you have felt challenged artistically, and mostly, inspired to create beautiful art of your own.

Please, don't let your learning stop here.
Find other artists who inspire you, and speak to your own style. There are many wonderful teachers out there who will have very valuable input to your journey as an artist.
You can only grow from here.

There is a wonderful community of watercolor artists who share their work online, (which you are now a part of!)
I encourage you to connect with others on a similar journey of learning so that you may bring encouragement and inspiration to each other's lives.

Feel free to share your art and progress with #amandahoustondesign, so I can follow along your journey.

Happy Painting!

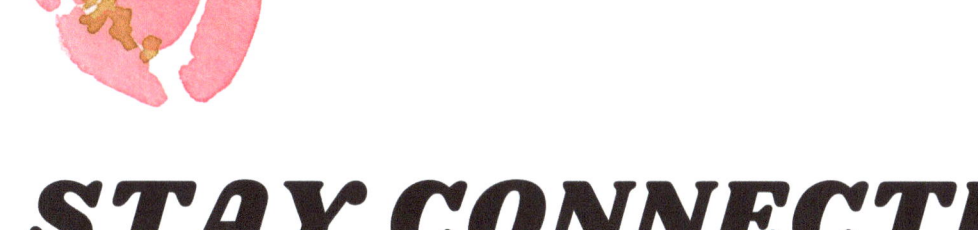

STAY CONNECTED

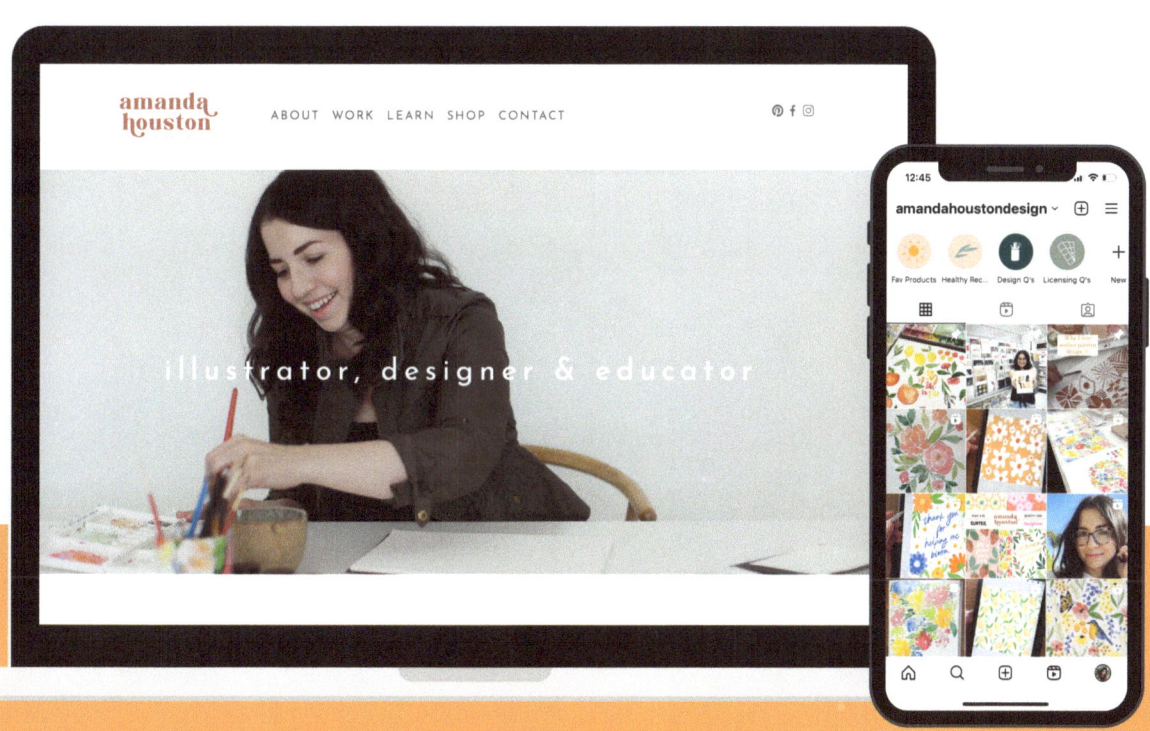

Find me online for more inspiration and art tips.
And check out my additional educational
resources to keep your creativity blooming!

CONTACT

www.amandahoustondesign.com   hello@amandahoustondesign.com   @amandahoustondesign